Kinloss Nursery Unit

The Smallest Christmas Tree

Words by PEGGY BLAKELEY   Paintings by MASAHIRO KASUYA

ADAM & CHARLES BLACK · LONDON

The READ TOGETHER Books
by Peggy Blakeley

Boy on a Hill Top
The Runaway Tram
Clouds
Holes
Neighbours
Jake
That Kind of Rabbit
Another Day Tomorrow
James and the Model Aeroplane
Emmie and Chips
I Bet I Could
The Little Shepherd Boy
The Day I Got Better
Rain
Oscar on the Moon
The Smallest Christmas Tree

A & C Black (Publishers) Limited
35 Bedford Row, London WC1R 4JH

© 1980 (English text) A & C Black (Publishers) Limited
© 1979 (illustrations) Shiko-sha Company Limited
First published in Japan by Shiko-sha Company Limited
Printed in Japan

ISBN 0 7136 2091 9

It was getting near to Christmas and
a little fir tree was standing
all alone on the hillside and he was weeping.
His little branches were drooping
and he was a sad sight.

A kindly bird was flying by
and he hovered above the little tree and asked
'Why are you crying?
Aren't you going to the town for Christmas?'
'No I'm not. They say I'm too small for Christmas,'
sobbed the little tree.

He told the bird how all his big brothers
had begged him to grow up quickly
and become a real Christmas tree
in time to go to the town.
And in the end they left him alone
and went to be Christmas trees themselves.

And so the little fir tree was lonely.
'Oh how I wish I was bigger,' he wept.
'Then I could have gone with the other fir trees
to be a Christmas tree.'

Hearing all this the bird became worried
and thought he should do something to help.
'In the town I have a friend, a donkey,
and he knows all about Christmas.
Perhaps he can help.'

And the bird flew away.

In a little while a fox passed by
on his way to town for Christmas.
The fox asked the little tree
why he was standing alone on the hillside.
And again the little fir tree
said he was too small to be a Christmas tree
and wept more bitter tears.

Meanwhile the little bird and his friend the donkey
were hurrying along towards the hillside.
'It's a long way,' brayed the donkey
'and I'm missing all the getting ready for Christmas in the town.'
And he grumbled as he trotted along.

'Here we are,' said the bird
as he landed by the tree.
And the donkey stared
for never had he seen such a little fir tree.

'Can I help you?' asked the donkey politely.
'Oh I wish I weren't so little.
I shall never be able to see Christmas in the town,'
sobbed the little tree.

'Don't cry, little tree,' said the donkey.
'Look, the lights are being lit
on the Christmas trees in the town.
Everybody is getting ready.
They're wrapping up presents
and hanging stockings by the fireplaces for Father Christmas.
They're getting the turkeys and the puddings ready
and soon the carol singing will begin.
Please don't cry little tree,' said the donkey.
'Perhaps next year you will have grown big enough
to see Christmas.'

So the little tree dried up his tears.
'Yes, maybe next year I'll be big enough.'
And he and the donkey and the bird went to sleep.

It was still and cold and quiet
and the snow began to fall.

And then it was Christmas Eve.
The snow glittered in the sun
and the world was all white.
And there amid the whiteness stood
the smallest and prettiest Christmas tree you could ever see.

'Away in a manger,
No crib for a bed,
The little Lord Jesus
Lay down his sweet head.'

The donkey and the bird started to sing
their favourite carol.

All the animals from near and far came to join in.

'The stars in the bright sky
Looked down where he lay,
The little Lord Jesus
Asleep on the hay.'

Soon everyone was gathered around
the smallest Christmas tree in the world.
And it was a starry snowy Christmas Eve
on the hillside.

Christmas had come to the little tree and
with so many friends around him,
he wasn't lonely any longer.

And then it was Christmas Day.
In the stable the baby Jesus lay sleeping
watched over by Joseph and Mary his mother.

And the little fir tree wasn't sad any more.
He'd had his own special Christmas on the hillside
with so many friends.
And trees, like babies, grow and he thought
he would be big enough by next year
to go to see Christmas in the town.